10711

D1255989

	DATE DUE	
JUN 01 2013		

The Urbana Free Library

To renew: call 217-367-4057
or go to "*urbanafreelibrary.org*"
and select "Renew/Request Items"

Shakira

Star Singer / Estrella de la canción

Zella Williams

PowerKiDS press. & **Editorial Buenas Letras**™
New York

Published in 2011 by The Rosen Publishing Group, Inc.
29 East 21st Street, New York, NY 10010

First Edition

Editor: Joanne Randolph
Book Design: Kate Laczynski
Photo Researcher: Jessica Gerweck
Spanish Translation: Eduardo Alamán

Photo Credits: Cover, pp. 1, 6–7, 15 Carlos Alvarez/Getty Images; p. 4 Dave M. Benett/Getty Images; p. 5 Francisco Leong/AFP/Getty Images; p. 8 Bertrand Parres/AFP/Getty Images; p. 9 Jeff Kravitz/FilmMagic/Getty Images; p. 10–11 Damian Duncan/Sony Music Archive/Getty Images; p. 12 Scott Gries/Getty Images; p. 13 Alexander Hassenstein/Getty Images; p. 14 Ronaldo Schemidt/AFP/Getty Images; p. 16 AFP/Getty Images; p. 17 Timothy A. Clary/AFP/Getty Images; pp. 18, 19 Shehzad Noorani/UNICEF via Getty Images; p. 21 Fotonoticias/Wireimage/Getty Images; p. 22 Juan Mabromata/AFP/Getty Images.

Library of Congress Cataloging-in-Publication Data

Williams, Zella.
  Shakira : star singer = Estrella de la canción / Zella Williams. — 1st ed.
    p. cm. — (Hispanic headliners = Hispanos en las noticias)
  English and Spanish.
  Includes index.
  ISBN 978-1-4488-0714-7 (library binding)
  1. Shakira—Juvenile literature. 2. Singers—Latin America—Biography—Juvenile literature. I. Title.
  ML3930.S46W54 2011
  782.42164092—dc22

2010015695

Manufactured in the United States of America

CPSIA Compliance Information: Batch #WS10PK: For Further Information contact Rosen Publishing, New York, New York at 1-800-237-9932

CONTENTS

CONTENIDO

If you ever listen to the radio, you have likely heard music by Shakira. She has recorded more than eight **albums**. She has also won many awards for her music. She is not busy only with her music, though. She is also known for her **charity** work. Shakira is a Latin American superstar!

Here Shakira sings at the MTV Europe Music Awards in Germany.

Aquí vemos a Shakira en los Premios de MTV Europa en Alemania.

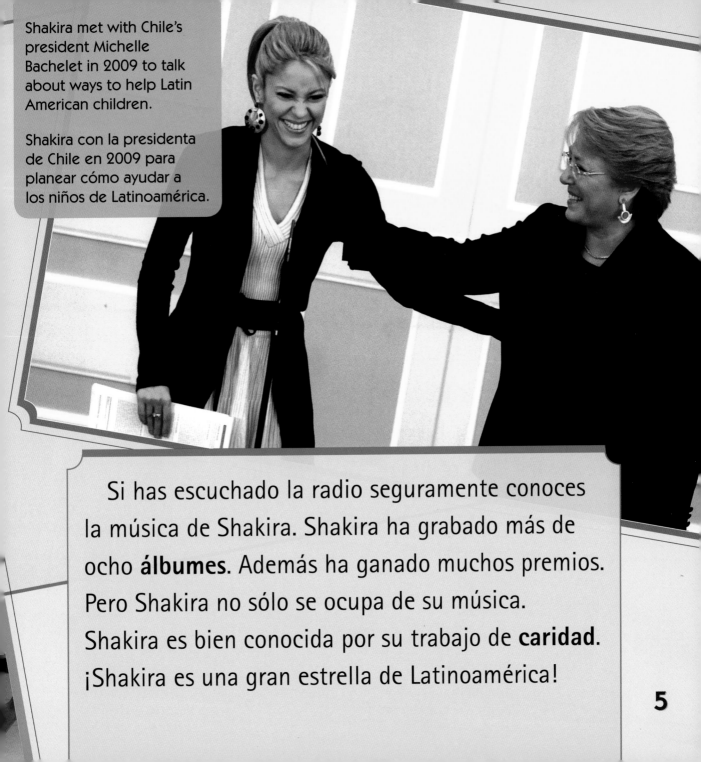

Shakira met with Chile's president Michelle Bachelet in 2009 to talk about ways to help Latin American children.

Shakira con la presidenta de Chile en 2009 para planear cómo ayudar a los niños de Latinoamérica.

Si has escuchado la radio seguramente conoces la música de Shakira. Shakira ha grabado más de ocho **álbumes**. Además ha ganado muchos premios. Pero Shakira no sólo se ocupa de su música. Shakira es bien conocida por su trabajo de **caridad**. ¡Shakira es una gran estrella de Latinoamérica!

Shakira Isabel Mebarak Ripoll was born in Baranquilla, Colombia, on February 2, 1977. Her father, William Mebarak Chadid, comes from a Lebanese family. He was born in New York but moved to Baranquilla as a baby. Her mother, Nidia Ripoll Torrado, was born in Baranquilla. Shakira's name means "full of grace" or "grateful."

Shakira's parents, shown here, are very proud of their daughter's hard work and success.

Aquí vemos a los padres de Shakira, muy orgullosos por los logros y el éxito de su hija.

Shakira Isabel Mebarak Ripoll nació en Barranquilla, Colombia, el 2 de febrero de 1977. El padre de Shakira, William Mebarak Chadid, viene de una familia libanesa. William nació en Nueva York pero de bebé se mudó a Barranquilla. Su mamá, Nidia Ripoll Torrado, nació en Barranquilla. El nombre de Shakira significa "llena de gracia".

Shakira went to **Catholic** school as a girl. She learned to read, write, and do math there. She also learned to sing and dance. This **education** did not happen in school, though. She showed her skill as a dancer at age seven. She jumped up and danced with a group of belly dancers at a Middle Eastern restaurant.

Shakira says that she always knew she would be a singer and songwriter, even when she was young.

Shakira dice que siempre supo que sería cantante o compositora.

Shakira has loved belly dancing since she was a child. She still uses it in her shows.

A Shakira siempre le gustó la danza del vientre y aún la utiliza en sus presentaciones.

De pequeña, Shakira asistió a una escuela **católica**. Ahí aprendió a leer y contar. También aprendió a cantar y a bailar. Pero esta **educación** no se dio en la escuela. A los siete años mostró gran habilidad para bailar. Shakira bailó con un grupo de bailarinas de la danza del vientre en un restaurante de comida de medio oriente.

9

Shakira recorded her first album at age 14. It did not sell very well. She kept trying, though. Her second album sold a little better, but Shakira was not happy. She felt that her first two recordings did not show who she was. Instead they showed who her producers thought she should be. She decided to change that in her next album.

Shakira is in the studio recording a song here.

Aquí, Shakira graba una canción en un estudio.

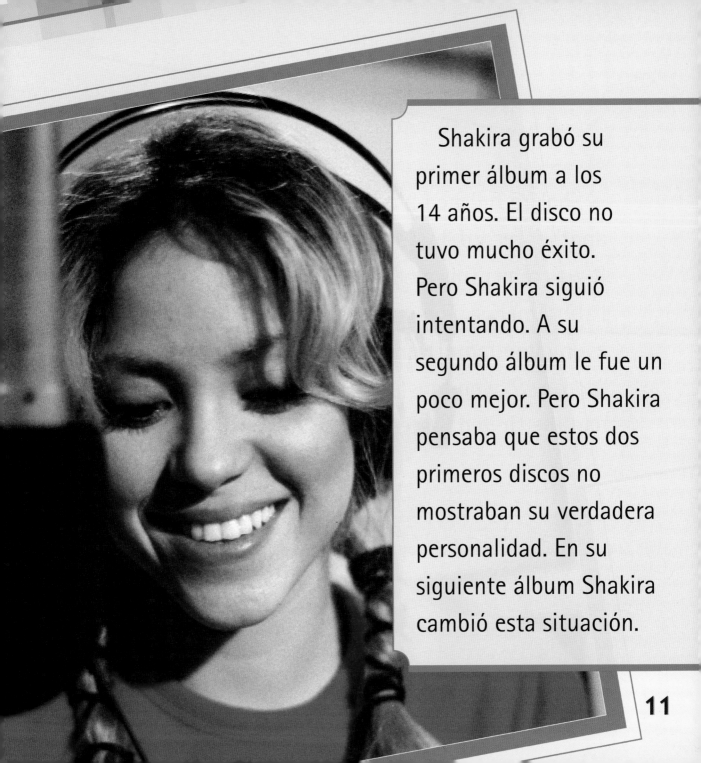

Shakira grabó su primer álbum a los 14 años. El disco no tuvo mucho éxito. Pero Shakira siguió intentando. A su segundo álbum le fue un poco mejor. Pero Shakira pensaba que estos dos primeros discos no mostraban su verdadera personalidad. En su siguiente álbum Shakira cambió esta situación.

Shakira finished high school before putting out another record. In 1995, *Pies Descalzos* came out. It was a hit! This album sold four million copies in Latin America. The stage was set for Shakira to gain even more fame. Her next album, *¿Dónde están los ladrones?*, won fans in France, Switzerland, Canada, and the United States.

Here Shakira sings at the 2006 Latin Grammy Awards.

Aquí vemos a Shakira cantando en los Premios Grammy a la música latina de 2006.

Shakira honors her Latino and Arab roots in her songs.

Shakira rinde homenaje a sus raíces árabes en sus canciones.

Shakira terminó la secundaria antes de producir su siguiente disco. En 1995 dio a conocer *Pies descalzos*. ¡El disco fue un éxito inmediato! Tan solo en Latinoamérica vendió 4 millones de copias. Su siguiente disco, *¿Donde están los ladrones?*, le ganó fanáticos en los Estados Unidos, Francia, Suiza y Canadá.

Shakira decided to try making an album in English. *Laundry Service* came out in 2001 and sold more than 13 million copies. She was now a worldwide star! Her next two albums did just as well. They both came out in 2005. Once again, her songs topped U.S. and Latin American music charts.

Shakira sang to a huge crowd in Mexico City. She has a lot of fans!

¡Shakira tiene muchos seguidores! Aquí la vemos en un concierto en la Ciudad de México.

One of Shakira's 2005 albums was in Spanish, and the other was in English.

En 2005, Shakira sacó un disco en inglés y otro en español.

Shakira decidió hacer un disco cantando en inglés. En 2001, *Laundry Service* vendió más de 13 millones de copias. Shakira se había convertido en una estrella mundial. Sus dos discos siguientes, en 2005, también tuvieron mucho éxito. Nuevamente alcanzó los primeros lugares en las listas de popularidad de Estados Unidos y Latinoamérica.

Shakira has done very well in her musical **career**. She wanted to give something back to her community. She started the Pies Descalzos **Foundation** in 1995. This foundation works to make sure poor children can get a good education and healthy food. It opened its first school in 2003, in Quibdó, Colombia.

Shakira is shown here at the opening of one of the six schools started by Pies Descalzos since 2003.

Aquí vemos a Shakira en 2003 en una de las seis escuelas comenzadas por Pies Descalzos .

Shakira ha tenido mucho éxito en su **carrera** y siempre ha querido dar algo a la comunidad. En 1995 comenzó la **fundación** Pies Descalzos. La fundación ayuda a que los niños de escasos recursos reciban buena educación, servicios de salud y comida. En 2003, abrió su primera escuela en Quibdó, Colombia.

Shakira has worked hard for education and the poor. In 2003, UNICEF made Shakira a goodwill **ambassador**. She is the youngest person to have served in this job. UNICEF works to make the lives of children better around the world. Shakira has gone to such countries as Spain, El Salvador, and Bangladesh for UNICEF.

In December 2007, Shakira visited a school in Teghor, Bangladesh, as part of her work with UNICEF.

Shakira visitó en 2007 una escuela en Tehhor, Bangladesh, como parte de su trabajo para UNICEF.

Here Shakira takes a walk with children who go to a UNICEF school in Rhajshahi, Bangladesh.

Aquí Shakira camina con chicos de una escuela de UNICEF en Rhajshahi, Bangladesh.

Shakira trabaja arduamente por la pobreza y la educación. En 2003, UNICEF la nombró **embajadora** de buena voluntad. Shakira es la persona más joven nombrada por UNICEF. UNICEF trabaja para mejorar la vida de los niños en el mundo. Shakira ha trabajado para UNICEF en países como España, El Salvador y Bangladesh.

Shakira is shown here reading with children during her visit to Bangladesh.

Shakira lee con varios chicos durante su visita a Bangladesh.

Shakira has won many awards for her music and her charity work. She has also been honored with Grammy Awards in the United States and Latin America. She has won many MTV Video Music Awards, too. She won the Billboard Spirit of Hope Award for her charity work.

In 2009, Shakira won two awards at the 40 Principales (Top 40) Awards in Spain.

En 2009, Shakira ganó dos premios en los Premios de los 40 Principales en España.

Shakira ha ganado muchos premios por su música y su trabajo de caridad. Ha ganado el premio Grammy Awards en los Estados Unidos y en Latinoamérica. También ha ganado el premio de los Videos MTV. Además ganó el premio Billboard Spirit of Hope por sus obras de caridad.

Shakira helped found ALAS in 2006. This is a group of Latin American artists and businesspeople who are working together to make early childhood education better in Latin American countries. She came out with another album in 2009, called *She Wolf*. There is sure to be more to come from this star singer!

En 2006, Shakira ayudó a fundar ALAS. Éste es un grupo de artistas empresarios latinoamericanos dedicados a mejorar la educación temprana en Latinoamérica. En 2009, Shakira presentó un nuevo álbum llamado *She Wolf*. ¡Seguramente será un éxito más en la carrera de esta cantante estrella!

GLOSSARY

albums (AL-bumz) Recordings or groups of songs.

ambassador (am-BA-suh-dur) Someone who is the voice for a country or group and who visits another country or group to share a message.

career (kuh-REER) A job.

Catholic (KATH-lik) Of the Roman Catholic faith.

charity (CHER-uh-tee) Giving to help the needy.

education (eh-juh-KAY-shun) Schooling or training.

foundation (fown-DAY-shun) A group set up to give help for a cause.

GLOSARIO

álbumes (los) Grabación de una o un grupo de canciones.

caridad (la) Dar ayuda a quienes lo necesitan.

carrera (la) Un trabajo.

católico, a Creyente de la religíon católica.

educación (la) Escuela o entrenamiento.

embajador, a (el/la) Una persona que representa a un país u organización y que visita a otros grupos o países para transmitir una misión o mensaje.

fundación (la) Una agrupación que se dedica a ayuda a una causa.

INDEX

ÍNDICE

WEB SITES / PÁGINAS DE INTERNET

Due to the changing nature of Internet links, PowerKids Press and Editorial Buenas Letras have developed an online list of Web sites related to the subject of this book. This site is updated regularly. Please use this link to access the list: www.powerkidslinks.com/hh/shakira/